THE UNINVITED GUEST

Overcoming the Power of Shame

Kenneth W. Chism

The Uninvited Guest

Overcoming the Power of Shame

by

Kenneth W. Chism

Copyright © 2024

ISBN: 979-8-9878331-6-2

Independently Published

First Edition

This book is dedicated to the loving memory of my mother, Zenobia M. Chism, and my spiritual father, Apostle Floyd E. Nelson, Sr. Your unwavering love, guidance, and wisdom have shaped me in more ways than words can express.

For helping make this book possible, I thank Aba Assiaw-Dufu, Dr. Rosemarie Downer, and Dr. Cedric L. Jennings.

Table of Contents

INTRODUCTION

O ne of my greatest heroes is the late South African president, Nelson Mandela. Following all the events of his life, it was an honor, upon my first visit to South Africa, to visit Mandela House in Soweto and the Mandela Museum. One of the highlights was visiting Robben Island, the prison where Nelson Mandela was wrongfully held in confinement for 18 of his 27-year sentence. Walking the grounds, through the halls, and seeing the cell where Mandela was confined left a major impact on my life. To serve time for a crime you did not commit is absolutely insane to me.

While on this tour, I had an extraordinary experience when I learned my tour guide was a former inmate of the prison. I thought, *you've got to be kidding me.* I asked him, "Sir, how in the world could you return to a place that once held you captive? Is it triggering? Does it make you feel embarrassed or shameful?"

He responded, "Shameful? Absolutely not! Shame has no power; it only grows if you feed it. What happens when you don't feed something? It eventually dies."

I pondered his response and thought about how many people are being defeated by what they've been feeding—shame. Think about it. All of us have felt shameful or embarrassed at some point in life. Whether it's shame from a failed marriage or relationship, getting fired from a job, or showing up to an all-white party and you didn't get the memo and wore blue. These examples are breeding grounds for shame, which can eventually cripple your life.

Shame often takes root in childhood. The devil, being a master deceiver, sows the seeds of shame when you're too young to know better or articulate how you feel. Over time, shame becomes an unconscious part of your identity. Without even realizing it, this hidden shame begins to affect your relationships and overall life.

Shame is like that annoying voice in your head persistently telling you something is fundamentally wrong with you. It makes you feel inadequate. This heavy feeling of unworthiness can make you believe you lack value, that people don't appreciate you. This can lead you to overcompensate for these imagined flaws or simply wave the red flag and quit.

Shame isn't something we're born with. It's something given to us or inflicted upon us. This can happen through emotional or physical abuse, character-damaging punishment, or verbal abuse loaded with negative messages.

Anaïs Nin once said, "Shame is the lie someone told you about yourself." Shame is like an uninvited guest that shows up without warning. We don't ask for it, but it sneaks in and makes itself comfortable. Soon, it's dictating how we should feel and think. However just like an unwanted guest, we need to kick shame out before it overstays its welcome.

We often beat ourselves up over the poor decisions we make and struggle to forgive ourselves and others. If you want to live free from shame, it is important to release the pain of your past to move forward.

When Mandela was released from prison, he said, "As I walked out the door toward the gate that would lead to my freedom, I knew if I didn't leave my bitterness and hatred behind, I'd still be in prison." How many of us have allowed shame to breed bitterness, hatred, and unforgiveness, thus keeping us imprisoned?

Have you wondered why some people achieve so much while others stay stuck in a cycle of pain? Where do you see yourself on this spectrum? Are you knee-deep in shame, or just wading through the shallow end? Knowing where you stand can pro-vide perspective on how far you need to go to get rid of it. Think of it as a GPS for your emotional well-being. You can't get to your destination without knowing your starting point.

I want this book to make you think and see just how much shame has stolen from you and the life God wants you to live. I want the next version of you to live shame-free and in pursuit of the goals you were once too afraid to chase.

As my tour guide at Robben Island said, shame only has power if we feed it. The first step to overcoming shame is acknowledging it. It takes courage to admit you're struggling with shame, but it's necessary to break free. Remember, we all have flaws, but they don't make us any less valuable or worthy of love.

In the following chapters, we'll explore the different ways shame can manifest, how it affects us, and how to overcome it. It's time to break free from the chains of shame and embrace a life of freedom and self-love. Are you ready to take this journey with me? Let's dive in.

1

SHAME: HOW DID YOU GET HERE?

Imagine this scenario. You're hosting a cozy dinner party with loved ones when suddenly, an unexpected guest shows up at your door. They weren't invited, but out of politeness, you allow them in. Before you know it, they've made themselves comfortable on your couch, and you find yourself catering to their needs. This unwelcomed guest now feels like a permanent fixture in your home. This is what shame feels like. It's the uninvited guest who sticks around and makes himself at home in your mind, constantly

making you feel unworthy and inadequate.

The powerful emotion of shame can have
a significant impact on our mental health
and well-being. It's often described as the
"master emotion" that leads to other negative emotions like anger, fear, guilt, and
sadness. Shame is also closely related to
low self-esteem and can erode our relationships with others. But where does
shame come from? And how can we deal
with this uninvited guest?

Shame is like an annoying guest who
shows up uninvited and refuses to leave.
It's subtle, sneaky, and before you realize
it, it's taken over your emotional "home." It
starts with small incursions—embarrassing moments, poor decisions, and
mistakes. Over time, these incidents, if not

addressed, snowball into a larger, more powerful emotion—shame.

Most of the time, we don't even recognize what we've opened the door to receive. Shame doesn't announce itself with grand theatrics. Instead, it slips in through the smallest cracks in our psyche. A harsh word from a loved one, a failure in front of peers, or even a casual comment on social media can trigger shame. These seemingly minor incidents accumulate, and before long, we find ourselves housing this unin-vited guest.

Once shame has settled in our lives, it starts to grow. We feed it with self-criti-cism, house it with our insecurities, and make it more comfortable with negative self-talk. It thrives on our fears and doubts, embedding itself deeper into our minds. And just like that, our house becomes its home, making it increasingly difficult to evict.

We all have had this uninvited guest show up on our doorstep and force its way into our lives. The key to managing shame begins with recognizing how it enters. Acknowledge feelings of inadequacy, the twinge of regret, or the sinking sensation in your gut. Identifying shame is the first step toward addressing it. Shame, like an uninvited guest, can be persistent and invasive. However, you don't have to allow it to take permanent residence in your life. By recognizing its presence and taking proactive steps, you can reclaim your emotional space and live a more self-compassionate, fulfilling life.

The Many Faces of Shame

Shame is a useless emotion, which kicks in when we become painfully self-aware of our perceived or imagined flaws. This often leads us to great lengths to hide these shortcomings. It creates a sense of self-perceived failure, either in your own eyes or in the eyes of others. The deep, overwhelming feeling of shame can consume you, making you feel unworthy of love and acceptance from those around you, or even from God. It is a complex emotion often stemming from guilt or feeling inadequate. Most times, it's confused with feelings like guilt and embarrassment, making it hard to fully determine what it really is.

Many people get stuck in a shame spiral, constantly replaying past mistakes and bad experiences. At the end of the day, shame adds no value to our lives and only hinders our personal growth.[1] Many people use shame and guilt interchangeably when they're not the same. They each affect us in different ways. Knowing how guilt and shame differ is key to dealing with them properly.

Shame Versus Guilt

Let's break down the difference between shame and guilt.[2] Feeling guilty involves thinking you've messed up and that it's your fault. Guilt is all about our behaviors and choices, those specific decisions and actions that leave us to fix them or apologize. Guilt says, "I made a mistake." Guilt acknowledges wrongdoing and is willing to address it. However, shame feels the need to hide the wrongdoing. Indeed, shame makes you feel like you're just not

good enough and worthless. It can inter-
fere with every part of your life. Shame is
like a dark cloud hanging over your head,
making you feel bad about yourself. Instead of simply acknowledging your
mistakes, correcting them, and moving on,
shame can make you feel like you are a
mistake.

The Origin of Shame

Shame is one of the first emotions mentioned in the Bible. The story kicks off in
the Garden of Eden with Adam and Eve.
They were just hanging out, living their
best lives. Everything was absolutely perfect until…bam! Eve was tempted by the
serpent and ate the forbidden fruit, which
she then shared with Adam. And just like
that, they gained both knowledge of good
and evil and a whole lot of shame. Their
sudden realization of being naked led to a

whirlwind of fear and a game of hide-and-seek.

However, let's be real here. Can you blame them? They were living in a perfect world, completely unburdened by any negative emotions or consequences. And then suddenly, they were hit with knowledge and shame all at once. Talk about overwhelming! We've all been there, right? That moment when you're hiding in your room because you accidentally broke your mom's favorite vase or when you blurted out something mean in the heat of an argument with someone you love and instantly regretted it. In moments like these, it can be easy to feel completely weighed down by our own flaws and shortcomings. Why do we feel this way? Maybe because, deep down, we believe we should've known better, or perhaps it's because our slip-up isn't exactly what society would call "acceptable."

Research shows that shame and guilt trigger different behaviors. [3] Shame makes us want to hide or run away, while guilt can incline us to fix things. Just like shame made Adam and Eve hide, it inclines us to do the same. If they had just said, "God, we're sorry," things might have turned out differently. But shame got in the way and stopped them from seeking God's forgiveness. How many times has this happened to you?

For Adam and Eve, a quick "sorry" could have led to God's unconditional love, forgiveness, and a fresh start. Instead, they got stuck in their shame, and now, we struggle with it too. The enemy's favorite trick is to make us feel ashamed, pulling us away from God's love and plan. We were created with a unique purpose. Shame is just a tool the enemy uses to stop us from fulfilling God's plan for our lives. Satan knows that if we remain distracted and bound by the shackles of shame, we won't be the blessing we were meant to be to others.

Not all shame comes from doing something wrong. Sometimes it can come just from embarrassing moments, like spilling coffee on someone or tripping in front of a crowd. Embarrassment is that awkward, self-conscious feeling you get when something happens in the moment and causes you to worry if others are judging or laughing at you.

Reimagine How You Think

As mentioned earlier, shame and guilt are two emotions we often mix up. They can invade our minds and affect us in different ways. This is especially true when it comes to receiving God's forgiveness. I truly believe it's possible for believers to reach a point where they move past sin or at least stop repeating the same mistakes again and again. However, as long as we're in our human bodies, we're all capable of slipping. There's a saying, "I'm not sinless, I just sin less."

I'm thankful that when we mess up, God's grace and forgiveness are readily available to us. Christ makes it possible for our sins to be forgiven. However, watch out! Shame can keep us from accepting God's amazing grace. Sometimes we struggle to forgive ourselves and feel unworthy of

God's grace and forgiveness. Have you ever had a moment when you made a mistake and felt the weight of it on your shoulders? Guilt sets in even though you've already repented and been forgiven. There's still this nagging feeling of guilt, like a red flag waving to remind you of your sin. This is the guilt Satan loves to throw at us. It's designed to keep us stuck in our past mistakes. It can be incredibly difficult to accept forgiveness when we are struggling with these feelings of guilt and unworthiness.

Now, shame is a whole different beast. While guilt is about seeing what you've done, shame is about seeing yourself as a failure because of what you've done. Think of guilt as putting the negative spotlight on the sin and shame as putting the negative spotlight on yourself. Unresolved guilt can easily evolve into a debilitating stronghold called shame. It all kicks off when we start internalizing guilt with thoughts like, "I did something bad." From there, our minds love to hit replay on whatever made us feel guilty in the first place. Do this long enough, and those negative thoughts dig in their heels and distort how we see ourselves. Without confronting the guilt and finding closure, it just lingers. In these instances, guilt has a sneaky way of turning into shame. Let's look at how this plays out.

Take some fellow named John, for example. He forgot his wedding anniversary, which left his wife seriously disappointed. He felt guilty and thought, *I should've remembered such an important date.* Instead of addressing it head-on, apologizing, and planning to make up to his wife, John avoided discussing the topic with her. Fast forward a bit. John's guilt took a dark turn, and he began thinking, *I am a terrible hus-band who doesn't deserve my wife's love and forgiveness because I should've known better.* And there you have it… his guilt snow-balled into full-blown shame. Remember, facing guilt head-on and finding a way to address it can stop it from growing into something far more damaging.

Here's a little wisdom from 2 Corinthians 10:4-5, "For the weapons of our warfare are not carnal, but mighty through God to the pulling down of strongholds; Casting down imaginations, and every high thing that exalteth itself against the knowledge of God, and bringing into captivity every thought to the obedience of Christ."

The imagination allows us to create fresh ideas and vivid pictures in our heads. However sometimes, those pictures aren't so pretty. The imagination can also create falsehoods; the most negative ideas and vivid images of ourselves. If you're seeing yourself as a failure, when you're actually a blood-washed child of God, then your imagination is playing tricks on you! Those images contradict how God sees you. It's a sneaky move by the devil to remind you of your slipups. Don't give guilt or shame the power to define you. You're more than your past mistakes! God's grace is bigger than any mistake we could ever make.

The Link Between Shame, Guilt, Anxiety and Anger

Shame and guilt are pretty interesting when you think about how they connect with other emotions, like anger and anxiety. [4] Research shows that, while both shame and guilt are connected to anxiety, shame is more strongly linked. [5] Also, shame and anger often go together, suggesting people who feel ashamed tend to blame others, leading to feelings of anger. This seems to alleviate some of the discomfort associated with feeling ashamed. [6] Shame is often linked to disgust because it involves rejecting your flawed self.[7] On the other hand, guilt kicks in when you break your moral code, and you feel responsible for any harm caused by your actions or inactions. Shame pops up when your ideal self-image and positive reputation take a hit.

It is crucial to recognize how damaging shame, guilt, and embarrassment can be. Once you understand how they hold you back, you can start breaking free and moving toward healing and restoration.

2

Shame: Sin or No Sin?

It's easy to think shame is always linked to doing something wrong, but that's not true. Sometimes, feeling embarrassed can also cause shame too. Just like the shame from sin, embarrassment can also keep you from moving forward. Embarrassment is a feeling of self-consciousness, shame, or awkwardness. When I was a kid, I used to stutter badly. It took me forever to get my words out, which was super embarrassing.

There were other times as a kid when I felt embarrassed, and sin had nothing to do with it. The first time this happened, I was about four years old. Looking back, it's pretty hilarious. My grandmother was a huge fan of Mr. Goodbar candy bars—you know, the ones with the bright yellow wrapper and shiny silver inside. To make them extra crunchy, she would put them in the freezer. One Saturday night, after grandma had already spoiled me with some Mr. Goodbar candy, my greedy self couldn't resist sneaking back to the freezer for more.

I thought I was grabbing another piece of Mr. Goodbar, but surprise, it was Ex-Lax—a laxative that looked and felt almost identical, just without the nuts. Clueless, I devoured it. Fast forward to Sunday morning. Church was in full swing, and my mother was seated in the choir, dressed in her pink and white robe, and I was seated up front where she could keep an eye on me. I was dressed to the nines, thanks to mom—sharp suit, shirt, and tie.

Suddenly, during the service, my stomach started rumbling—not the Holy Ghost kind of rumble. It was a code-red, emergency type of rumble. *Oh no*, I thought, *this can't be happening*. I had no clue that the Ex-Lax was the culprit. To make matters worse, I've always been squeamish about using public restrooms. Nonetheless, there I was, my stomach doing flips and needing the restroom badly. I squirmed in my seat, but I could hear my mom saying, "You sit right here and don't you dare move—or else." Listen, I knew momma meant exactly what she said.

However, with what was going on in my stomach, I decided to face the consequences of disobeying mom. I rushed downstairs to the restroom. Unfortunately, I didn't make it in time. Yep, you guessed it. The worst happened. Of course, mom followed me out and found out what happened. Talk about feeling embarrassed, wow! Service was over by that point, and I ended up having to wear my mother's choir robe home because my clothes were soiled. Can you imagine the embarrassment?

I was so embarrassed for using the bathroom on myself because I made the innocent mistake of eating Ex-Lax. Oh, and let's not forget my fear of using public restrooms. Now, picture this. A young boy, wrapped in a pink and white choir robe, making the humiliating walk from the church to his mother's car. All the other kids were laughing at me and calling me names. It was just horrible. That day, I felt the weight of embarrassment, shame, and guilt all at the same time.

My second encounter hit me around the age of six. The memory of it still stands out like a sore thumb. I can still picture it vividly. An altar call was given at my church specifically for kids born out of wedlock. The idea was to gather us together and pray for our well-being. During this experience, we were labeled as "bastards," a word with which I was unfamiliar until that moment. This experience really emphasized the notion that we were considered inferior to the other kids born through marriage. This label had a lasting impact on my self-esteem and self-worth. I felt like an outsider and to constantly questioned my worth as a human being. It also made me realize the harmful effects of labeling and how it can perpetuate discrimination and prejudice. While I truly believe the preacher had good intentions and didn't mean any harm, I quickly learned that good intentions without wisdom can sometimes backfire.

Here I am, standing at the altar with two other kids, all of us made a spectacle because of how we came into the world. As a kid, I did not have the full agency to express how I felt in that moment. However, I knew it didn't feel good at all. It made me feel like there was something wrong with me, like I was an accident. The worst part was walking back to my seat while all the other kids giggled and pointed fingers. This incident was particularly mortifying because it happened in front of the same group of children who had previously laughed at me for using the bathroom on myself.

This painfully awkward moment wasn't due to any sin on my part. Instead, it was more a reflection of the ignorance around me. Back in the day, being born out of wedlock was the church's big scandal—kind of like how they handle hot topics like abortion or LGBTQIA+ issues now. This belief haunted me for years. It has been a long and tough journey to reach a place of solace. For years, I struggled with feeling like I didn't measure up simply because of the circumstances of my birth. It was as if an invisible scoreboard kept track of everything I lacked compared to my peers. These shortcomings seemed to cling to me like an embarrassing nickname that just wouldn't die. I mean, come on, who hasn't felt the sting of not measuring up at some point in their life? The difference is when you're young, those feelings are magnified a thousandfold. It's like you're living under a giant magnifying glass, and every little remark or giggle is a scorching ray piercing through your sense of self-worth. I remember vividly how a casual chuckle from across the playground could trigger me into a spiral of overwhelming self-doubt. "Are they laughing at me? Did I do something wrong?"

Nonetheless, I eventually broke free from those feelings of not being enough. And it wasn't like some magical, overnight transformation. It took years of self-reflection, and yes, a few awkward encounters with the reality of who I truly am—but I got there, and you can too!

One of the biggest turning points for me was realizing my self-worth and understanding who God created me to be. It was like someone turned on a light switch, illuminating all the dark corners where my insecurities hid. I had to decide to believe I was not a mistake, that my life has purpose. This wasn't easy, mind you. It's like trying to convince yourself that squash taste good after a lifetime of hating it. Needless to say, with time, I started to see myself through a different lens. I began to recognize the very circumstances I once saw as my downfall were actually the building blocks of my resilience and character. It was a shift from seeing myself as a victim of my circumstances to seeing myself as a survivor and a thriver.

No matter where you come from or what your background is, people will have their opinions and doubts about your potential. Here's the deal. God's plan and purpose for your life will always manifest in the end. Even Jesus wasn't spared from harsh judgment. People questioned His legitimacy due to the circumstances of his birth and even wondered, "Can anything good come from Nazareth?" Yet, His life proved otherwise. In the same way, your background or family history does not determine your worth or potential.

Jesus came from humble beginnings, born to a carpenter and growing up in a small town. Despite this, He went on to change the world and inspire people through His teachings and actions. This just goes to show our past does not define us. However, our actions and choices shape who we are.

It's crucial to understand that if you don't shake off self-doubt and appreciate your worth, you'll keep seeing yourself as a mistake. Believe me, you are not a mistake. You're woven into the very fabric of God's plan. He orchestrated your parents' union, marital status notwithstanding, because He intended for you to exist. God is the ultimate Creator of life, and if He didn't want you here, you wouldn't be. Just as I'm not a mistake, neither are you. You were purposefully and lovingly crafted in the mind of God.

"I praise you because I am fearfully and wonderfully made; your works are wonderful, I know that full well."[8] This verse highlights the incredible worth each of us has, emphasizing we were purposely created by God, not by accident. Even when we see our flaws, God sees a work of art in progress. He already knows the good plans He has for us, as mentioned in Jeremiah 29:11.

From God's viewpoint, these plans are already fulfilled. Hence, there's no need for shame or feelings of inadequacy. Let's take a moment to reflect on this. The same God who created the vast, breathtaking universe also intentionally formed each one of us. That's something worth marveling at! And not only did He create us, but He also continues to work in our lives, guiding and shaping us into who we are meant to be.

3

SHAME: THE SILENT ENEMY

Shame is one of the most powerful and destructive emotions we can experience. It has the ability to warp our self-image, self-worth, and even our outlook on life. When caught in the grip of shame, it leaves you feeling defeated and an easy target for control and manipulation. This vicious cycle can make anyone feel like they're never good enough and unworthy of living up to their full potential. It ultimately wreaks havoc on our ability to build healthy relationships and pursue goals.

Keep in mind, shame isn't always self-inflicted. It can be imposed by external forces, such as families, religious institutions, and other social structures you would least expect. These forces have used shame as a tool to control behavior and enforce conformity for ages.

Family members can be some of our biggest fans and, sometimes, our toughest critics, especially in cultures where reputation is everything. Parents might throw shade if you don't ace those exams, stick to family traditions, or follow their dream career for you. Ever been at a family gathering and had a relative make a snide comment about your life choices? You're a graphic designer, but Aunt Carol thinks you should've been a doctor or a lawyer. Or have you've chosen not to tie the knot? Brace yourself for the, "Oh, but you'll be so lonely!" pity party.

Religious institutions often play the shame game in order to enforce moral codes and behavior norms. Ever missed a service or had your name placed on the church bulletin board for not paying tithes? They'll try to control everything from who you love to what you wear. And society? It's got this bizarre fixation on squeezing everyone into a particular mold. Don't fit into society's ideal body image? Get ready for some serious body shaming. Feel like a loser because you didn't purchase a house by age 30 or not pulling in a six-figure salary? I guess the world may see you as an even bigger loser. Society imposes this checklist of goals, and if you're not checking the boxes, shame can sneak up on you. When people make you feel ashamed, it can make you feel inadequate and cause anxiety or even depression. Sometimes, it can drive you to really harmful actions.

The consequences of shame on personal development are extensive. The real harm lies in how shame can infiltrate the core of our psyche, seeping into our thoughts and beliefs. Before you know it, shame, the uninvited guest, will gradually erode your self-esteem and sense of worth. Shame's impact on self-worth is enormous. It undermines confidence and prevents people from recognizing their value and potential. If you let it, shame will bleed into every part of your life, influencing your thoughts, actions, and relationships.

Shame can be paralyzing. This destructive emotion can significantly affect your mental health and stunt your personal growth. Shame is fueled through personal experiences, religious teachings, family dynamics, cultural norms, and societal pressures, providing plenty of opportunities to cause harm.

The Early Formation of Shame

Shame often ties back to our childhood and early experiences with our parents. From the moment we're born, we start figuring out who we are and how the world works. This process, of course, is substantially influenced by our primary caregiver. Even with two parents in the picture, children usually have that one go-to person to which they cling.

During these early years, children are like sponges, soaking up everything and depending on their caregivers for emotional support, validation, and guidance. How parents react to their child's behaviors and feelings hugely impacts the child's self-esteem and emotional well-being. When parents show consistent love, support, and understanding, those children typically develop a healthy sense of self-worth and learn to manage their emotions effectively.

Remember my experience at the church altar for children born out of wedlock? After that service, my mom prayed over me during our drive home. She kept reaffirming my identity and faith. Anyone who knew her knew she was serious about prayer and her baby. I don't know if she ever had words with the church leaders about that altar call. All I know is that another invitation to the altar like that was never extended again. My mom was intentional in countering the effects of my unfortunate altar experience through prayer and positive affirmations. She always knew God's hand was upon my life, and daily, she declared, "The seed of the righteous is blessed." While helpful, my mother's emotional and spiritual support didn't exclude me from Satan's attacks. His job was to dismantle and destroy every affirming prayer, prophesy, and word spoken over my life. Yes, I was blessed with a praying mother and grandmother, but I still had to believe God's Word for myself.

When I became a teenager, I quickly realized my relationship with God had to be personal. I was grateful for the solid foundation my mother and grandmother had laid in my life. However, I needed to develop my own relationship with Jesus. There comes a point in your life when the Lord will reveal Himself to you personally. The relationship shifts from hearing about God to truly knowing God.

On the other hand, when parents respond to their children's behaviors with criticism, rejection, or neglect, those children may very well internalize shame. For example, if a child is constantly scolded or ridiculed for expressing their emotions or making mistakes, they may start to believe there's something inherently wrong with them. Over time, these negative experiences can turn into deep feelings of inadequacy, unworthiness, and shame.

Parents who set unrealistically high expectations for their children can contribute to feelings of shame. When children feel pressured to meet these standards and repeatedly fall short, they may start to think they're not good enough. This sense of failure can lead to lasting feelings of shame and self-doubt well into adulthood.

It's also important to note that parents can pass shame on to their children without even realizing it. Many parents carry around their unresolved shame and unintentionally transfer it to their children. Plus, societal norms and cultural values play a big part in shaping how parents deal with shame. The long-lasting effects of early shaming incidents can take a toll on someone's sense of self. However, remember we are cherished by the Most High God and seen as whole and complete, regardless of our family background and upbringing.

By recognizing the origins of shame and how it affects children's development, parents can help cultivate emotional well-being and resilience in their children. With loving and supportive parenting, we can break the shame-cycle and raise children who feel worthy, valued, and capable.

Shame in Places We Least Expect It

Shame is a sneaky beast, creeping into places where we least expect it. Take the church, for example—the place where you'd think compassion and inclusivity would reign supreme. Yet, shame can thrive there too, often fueled by stereotypes and deep-seated biases. This mix of human relationships, religious beliefs, and societal inequalities show up within different denominations and congregations.

The church, meant to be a haven of love and understanding, can sometimes turn into a breeding ground for shame. Ever questioned your faith? In some churches, expressing doubt can lead to whispers behind your back or, worse, an outright sermon aimed directly at your "lack of faith." Instead of addressing your concerns, you're made to feel wrong for even thinking about them.

People often feel like they must be perfect while handling their own battles. Stereotypes, misinterpretations of Scripture, and deep-rooted societal and religious beliefs add more shame. When someone is marginalized, stereotypes make them feel lesser and ashamed. These labels mess with their self-image and change how others view and treat them.

Inequality within religious settings can manifest in various forms, impacting individuals and groups differently based on their gender, ethnicity, socioeconomic status, and other factors. Even when we observe these inequalities, those burdened by shame often hide out of fear of rejection. This only magnifies the negative impact of shame. By shining a spotlight on the destructive power of shame and challenging stereotypes within religious communities, the church can work toward building a more inclusive and compassionate environment. This way, people can feel empowered to share their vulnerabilities willingly and seek support without fear of judgment.

When driven by stereotypes, shame perpetuates inequalities. People who internalize these prejudices might believe their worth is diminished or that they're inherently flawed, which can lead to self-blame and self-sabotage. Shame can also act as a barrier to seeking help or accessing resources, making disparities even worse.

To tackle this issue, it is important for faith communities to break down stereotypes, encouraging open and honest conversations about shame, and foster environments where everyone feels valued and welcomed. This involves education, empathy, and a willingness to question deep-seated beliefs and behaviors. Faith leaders play a key role in nurturing an inclusive and compassionate church environment. This doesn't entail straying from core beliefs. Instead, it involves loving God and loving your neighbor as you love yourself. This mindset embraces the diversity and humanity of all people, regardless of differences.

4

SHAME AND THE CHURCH

Again, shame isn't always due to sin or wrongdoing. However, many people stop going to church because they feel embarrassed by their choices, mistakes, and failures. They may have experienced significant life changes like divorce, having a baby outside of marriage, or being criticized for not following a specific dress code. Sometimes, people leave because others unfairly impose their own strict beliefs and standards, making them feel like they can never measure up. The fear of judgmental looks and harsh comments from pastors and fellow congregants can make returning to church very difficult.

There was a time when women who got pregnant outside of wedlock had to stand in front of the church, ask for forgiveness, and cease participating in church activities until after their baby was born. Meanwhile, the men involved usually didn't face any such consequences. I've always thought that the church's unfair response, in this regard, is incredibly sexist and hypocritical. Clearly, she couldn't get pregnant by herself, right?

I've had many conversations with people who left their local assembly and never returned just because they had failed to adhere to a strict standard or dress code. Women who wore pants, red lipstick, or who did not wear a head-covering were often frowned upon and shamed. Picture this. A woman visits a church for the first time, looking for hope and a word of encouragement. Instead, her appearance is scrutinized as if she should have known and adhered to that church's specific dress code. If her dress is deemed too short or if she's wearing pants, she's singled out and made to wear a choir robe or, even worse, have a sheet wrapped around her waist, despite being a visitor. And yes, this is a true story. Seriously, how much hope or encouragement can you expect to find when you're being embarrassed like that? Again, none of these instances were linked to sin or wrongdoing.

Back in the early 1990s, I had become a more fashion-conscious young guy. I wanted to add some color to my wardrobe instead of sticking to the usual black, brown, navy, or gray suits. I always thought of myself as a bit of a fashion trail-blazer. I remember rocking bright blazers to church—red, purple, royal blue. What was I thinking? The looks, the stares, and the harsh comments were off the charts. "You shouldn't wear those colors, You're a man, and it's not appropriate." Seriously? These comments were all based on their personal beliefs and opinions, which made me second-guess my fashion choices, lead-ing me to conform to how they wanted me to dress. It didn't matter that I was faithful in my church duties and serving God. Just stick with the dark, basic colors; it's more modest and masculine. Church folk also extended their micro-aggressions to my relationships and subsequent marriage.

I met this incredible girl through my church organization. We were both in our early 20s. Not only is she beautiful, but we hit it off on so many levels—from music and fashion to our shared love for God. We quickly became best friends. Over time, our bond deepened into something truly special. I loved her and treasured every moment we spent together, even though she lived in New York.

As the years went by, my feelings for her grew stronger. However, I was unsure of what to do. There was never a question of my love for her. Dreaming of marriage and a family was one thing. Knowing how to make it work was another story. Since my parents were never married, I didn't have a real-life example to follow. The church seemed more focused on getting people hitched than on teaching them how to build a successful marriage and relationship. They'd say, "It is better to marry than to burn," but didn't provide the tools to sustain a marriage. According to the church, the next step for me was simply to get married.

When I sought advice from a former pastor about how I was feeling, he said I needed a wife and should get married soon since I was entering the ministry. Whether I was in love or not—it didn't matter; he assured me falling in love would eventually come later. Not exactly the guidance I expected to hear.

Fast forward to our wedding day, which was like a fairytale—beautiful flowers, heartfelt vows, teary-eyed guests—it had all the emotions. Once the honeymoon phase was over, reality hit me really hard. It felt like crashing into a brick wall. I began questioning every decision which had led me to that point. Did I make the right choice? Is this what I truly wanted for my life right now? It felt like I was living someone else's life. Doubts about my self-worth and whether I could actually make the marriage work overwhelmed me. Questions about my sexuality from other people added another layer of complexity to my already chaotic thoughts. The fear and doubt were almost paralyzing.

Eventually, I had to confront these feelings. Ignoring them wasn't fair to me or my then wife. Coming to terms with my emotions was one of the hardest things I've ever done. Sometimes, you have to make tough decisions and be honest with yourself.

By 2005, after five years of marriage, it was over. Five years might not seem like a long time, but it was long enough for me to realize I wasn't ready for marriage. There was no infidelity or a major issue that ended it, just my own feelings of insecurities. Despite the support from my ex-wife and our families, the feeling of not being enough drowned out their voices. I felt like a total failure, not only letting not just myself down but also disappointing my ex-wife. Looking back, I realize shame can seriously affect your relationships. I wanted to be married, but I wasn't emotionally or spiritually ready. I could have stayed married to avoid the awkwardness of divorce, but deep down, I knew it wasn't right.

While I was married, I had also received the call to pastor, which made this period of my life even more complicated. How was this going to work? Did the Lord change His mind now that I'm no longer married? How would I be received as a divorced pastor? How would I counsel married or engaged couples? This was all too much for me to deal with at one time.

The decision to divorce wasn't easy at all. To make matters worse, the teachings of my church regarded divorce as a big NO. It felt like I was going straight to hell in gasoline drawls. The church folks didn't make it any easier with their rumors and gossip. However, all of this was necessary for me to find my path and be true to myself of what I actually wanted. In the end, clarity came through the chaos. I learned so much about myself in the process. One of the greatest things I learned is, knowing yourself is key. In your 20s, you're still figuring out who you are. By your 30s, what you thought you wanted often changes. Honestly, I should've taken the time to reflect and pray before saying, "I do." Ultimately, know yourself and your true desires before committing to another person.

Sometimes you have to lose yourself to find yourself. Life has a funny way of teaching us lessons. My divorce taught me the importance of being honest with myself and facing my fears head-on. If you're going through something similar, know that it's okay to question, doubt, and ultimately choose what's best for you.

Reflecting on the past, I believe it's important for people to love themselves and develop into well-rounded individuals, while seeking God's guidance. This is helpful to do especially before making big decisions like marriage. Also, if we do this and make room for godly advice, the church's divorce rate would be lower. Being told, "You have the Holy Ghost, so make it work," isn't helpful or godly counsel. Instead, it shows that the person giving advice likely doesn't know how to make it work or is struggling in their marriage themselves. Let's focus on helping individuals love and appreciate being single, rather than treating singleness like some kind of curse. This approach can prevent unhappy lives, miserable marriages, and broken families. Pushing people into marriage because of their age, ministry title and demands, or any other societal pressures is a recipe for disaster.

After being divorced for nearly 20 years, my ex-wife and I are still the best of friends. We owe a lot to our families who have always supported us and ensured we never felt awkward or ashamed. Believe me, not every breakup has to be messy and filled with anger. When you have self-awareness and God's love guiding you, things can turn out much differently.

When I was going through this rough patch, God sent an authentic man of faith into my life. I had respected other pastors before, but this man was different. It felt like God had sent me a shepherd who truly understood what I needed. He didn't judge me or point out my mistakes. Instead, he lovingly corrected me and caused me to rethink my decisions that led me on a new path. He really listened, offered godly advice, showed me grace and encouraged me along the way. His way of ministering was so unique—no long lectures or condemnation, just pure love and heartfelt understanding. That experience changed my life and restored my faith in church leadership.

That man later became my pastor, the late Apostle Floyd E. Nelson, Sr. Through his leadership, he guided me to healing and wholeness, by not only treating my symptoms but also by helping me identify the root cause of my shame. This brought me the deliverance I needed to break free from shame and guilt.

When I reflect on my time growing up in the church, I can't help but remember the church being much more strict compared to now. It can be argued the church has made some strides in many areas. However, the harm from past actions has left a lasting impact on countless people who've experienced similar, if not worse, experiences as I did while growing up in the church. These actions planted seeds of shame right within God's house. The church should serve as a spiritual hospital that promotes healing, not a place inflicting pain. It's time for the church to face its mistakes, and take responsibility for the harm it has caused. Acknowledging the past and making amends are critical for moving forward. The church is called to make a real impact on people's lives by sharing God's love.

Even though I'm sharing stories based on real events I have witnessed and experienced, they don't diminish my belief in the church. I want to make it clear—I am not bitter or angry with the church. In fact, I love the church and fully support the true mission of the Church of Jesus Christ. The church continues to be an important and meaningful and impactful part of my life today. It's still a place to find healing and spiritual renewal. By owning up to our mistakes and working together, we can show the world what it really means to be the church through reconciliation and God's transformative, healing power to those who need it.

5

JESUS, THE SHAME BREAKER

In Micah 2:13, Jesus is portrayed as the breaker, the One who leads us out of bondage. He comes to shatter barriers and cycles, setting captives free. Jesus' ultimate act of love on the cross goes beyond forgiving sins and healing diseases. It includes breaking shame and defeating every evil scheme of the enemy.

The perfect and finished work of Calvary is the ultimate demonstration of Jesus' love for us. He sacrificed His life on the cross to offer salvation and redeem humanity with His blood. His sacrifice was flawless. He nailed it, literally fulfilling His mission as our blessed Savior. There's no need for Him to make a repeat trip to the cross for our mistakes because again, it is finished.

This mind-blowing truth means everything. Our past, present, and future are wrapped up in His ultimate sacrifice for us, which is all covered by His love and forgiveness. So, there's no reason to be afraid or to hide from God when we mess up. We can approach Him with confidence, knowing His forgiveness is available to us. It's all under His blood!

The writer of Hebrews reminds us, "For we do not have a high priest who is unable to empathize with our weaknesses, but we have one who has been tempted in every way, just as we are—yet he did not sin."⁹ That being said, know that Jesus has faced everything you and I have or will ever face in this life—every emotion, struggle, pain, loss, and even addiction. He faced every temptation and overcame it blamelessly and without sinning. He serves as our model, showing us that overcoming temptations is possible when we operate totally in His strength, and not our own.

Jesus, God's only begotten son, experienced abandonment for us. "For he hath made him to be sin for us, who knew no sin; that we might be made the righteousness of God in him." ¹⁰ He didn't just become sin for us—He took our place on the cross. Jesus faced shame, sin, and rejection on our behalf and overcame them all so that we can too.

Another one of my favorite scriptures is Hebrews 12:2: "Looking unto Jesus the author and finisher of our faith; who for the joy that was set before him endured the cross, despising the shame, and is set down at the right hand of the throne of God." [11] People often miss an important part of this scripture. That is, Christ despised the shame. What does that really mean? Despising is the same as disregarding it or not paying attention to it.

When we think about the crucifixion, it's easy to focus solely on the physical pain Jesus endured. However, consider the other aspects of His sufferings, like the shame and disgrace associated with the cross. Imagine being beaten and then put on display naked and exposed before everyone you know—friends, family, coworkers. How would you feel? In the Roman world, crucifixion wasn't just about inflicting physical pain. It was designed to publicly humiliate and degrade. Paintings and sculptures often show Jesus with a cloth around His waist. However, the Romans actually stripped Him completely naked. Jews saw the human body as sacred and detested the naked idols of pagan cultures. So being stripped naked was the height of shame and disgrace.

Jesus chose to ignore this shame and faced it head-on like the true G.O.A.T. (Greatest of All Time) He is. He didn't allow it to define His purpose or sway His resolve. Instead of letting shame conquer Him, He conquered it by simply not acknowledging it. Imagine that! Choosing to rise above the most intense form of public humiliation imaginable.

Think about the last time you felt ashamed. Did it help you in any way? Did it make you stronger, wiser, or happier? Probably not. Shame is a useless emotion and has a way of paralyzing us, making us feel small and insignificant. Yet, Jesus showed us it doesn't have to be this way.

If we believe Isaiah 53:5 that by His stripes we are healed, we must also believe He paid the price for shame. Why live with it if Christ died to abolish it? Your freedom from shame is closely tied to your faith in His sacrifice. Without faith in Christ's redemptive power, you will find yourself stuck in shame, guilt, and self-condemnation.

Until you fully accept and believe in God's promises, you'll be trapped by others' opinions and live in their judgments. Having faith in what Christ provided on the cross can help us truly break free from shame and walk in the freedom and love

He offers. Hebrews 11:6 emphasizes this key point, stating that "…it is impossible to please God without faith. Anyone who wants to come to him must believe that God exists and that He rewards those who sincerely seek Him."[12]

The most intense battle we face is within our minds. Our thoughts and beliefs shape our reality. "For as a man thinketh in his heart, so is he." We often give too much power to others' opinions, letting their words influence our self-perception and circumstances. We often overlook the profound truth within God's Word. God's truth is not defined by others' opinions but only by His Word. Say this out loud with me, "God told the truth about me, and that's what I choose to believe." Let this declaration liberate you from others' opinions in Jesus' name.

Overcoming negative thoughts and others' opinions is based on how you choose to respond to them. Your response should be rooted in the Scriptures, not just echoing what everyone else says. If you rely on God's Word, you're anchoring yourself in absolute truth because His Word is rock-solid. The Scriptures aren't just words on a page. They reflect God's very nature and His thoughts about you. Remember, God is not a man, so He does not lie.[13]

By ignoring the shame of the cross, Jesus demonstrated that our worth isn't tied to how others perceive us. It's not about the labels that society throws our way or the mistakes we've made. Our worth comes from who we are at our core and the purpose we serve.

This perspective is liberating. If Jesus can ignore the ultimate form of shame, then surely, we can overlook the shame we encounter in our daily lives. Maybe it's a mistake at work, an awkward social interaction, or a personal failure that has brought shame into your life. Whatever it is, it doesn't have to define you.

In essence, Jesus' example of ignoring shame teaches us a powerful lesson. We can choose to rise above others' judgments and criticisms, by focusing on our God-given purpose and potential. After all, shame is just an emotion that loses its grip the moment we decide to ignore it. Once we fully accept what Christ has done for us through the cross, we can hold our heads high, live without shame, and fully realize our divine purpose.

Will the True Church Please Stand Up

Most people believe that the church is supposed to be a place of refuge, where you can come in heavily burdened and come out lighter and more hopeful. Let's be honest, how often does it really happen? The real church should be where you can bring your worries without judgment and get the support you need to face life's challenges. And no, I'm not just talking about the cookies and coffee in the fellowship hall (though those are important too).

When Jesus established His Church, He had a very clear vision. It was all about relationship, not religion or just keeping a bunch of rules. Think about it. His finished work on Calvary wasn't about creating a new set of dos and don'ts. It was about restoring the broken fellowship between God and man. One of the first passage of scriptures I memorized as a child was John 3:16-17: "For God so loved the world, that he gave his only begotten Son, that whosoever believeth in him should not perish, but have everlasting life. For God sent not his Son into the world to condemn the world; but that the world through him might be saved."[14] Now, that's still good news to me!

The best part of this message is anyone can be saved. We don't get to choose who receives salvation, and we certainly don't get to exclude anyone. So, what about condemnation? Well, it doesn't come from Christ. He didn't show up to point fingers or make us feel ashamed. He came to offer a lifeline, a way out of the mess we face in our lives. This is the core of Christianity!

The church was designed to be a place to find safety and comfort during hard times.

Sadly, somewhere along the way, the true purpose of the church has been overshadowed by a culture of superficiality and judgment. It's almost like a bad reality TV show in which everyone is trying to outdo each other in the "holier-than-thou" department. This environment tends to manufacture phonies. Those dealing with shame, rejection, and condemnation become inclined to mask their pain instead of seeking the help they need.

For some inexplicable reason, once we receive salvation and God's grace, many Christians act as if God stopped being gracious, like His forgiveness is no longer available to others. It's as if we believe the divine grace tap has been turned off right after it reached us.

I'm convinced that most believers seem to suffer from spiritual amnesia. They overlook the journey God has guided them through and the challenges He has helped them overcome. These same people are often the main ones who judge others, making them feel unworthy of receiving God's love.

Here's the kicker. I've found that the people who are most judgmental are usually dealing with something themselves. This self-righteous, holier-than-thou disposition is just a facade or smokescreen to keep their issues hidden from others. It's easier to judge someone else when you think their struggle is more visible. Meanwhile, you're able to conceal your issues because they are matters of the heart—pride, envy, jealousy, or lying to yourself and pretending you have it all together. Ma'am or sir? Let's be honest. We're all dealing with something, hence our need for Jesus. He's still working on all of us.

When Jesus came, He made it clear that His focus was on reaching out to sinners and those who were imperfect. He said "Those who are well have no need of a physician, but those who are sick. I have not come to call the righteous, but sinners to repentance."[15] We should be able to be honest about our emotional state and not be judged. Instead, those who are stronger in faith should help restore the broken with gentleness.[16]

People are searching for hope and answers. Guess what? That's where the body of Christ comes in. We need to be open about our struggles and find comfort in God's presence and our faith community. Let's value authenticity, show vulnerability, and welcome the broken-hearted with open arms. Picture a community where anyone can show up as they are, without fear of judgment, and receive the love and support they need. That's what the real church should look like. Let's stop making it difficult for people to encounter Jesus and instead share our stories of how we've been redeemed by Christ's love. By doing so, we can tear down walls of judgment and build bridges of forgiveness and understanding.

6

FROM THE INSIDE OUT

You might think: If only I landed that dream job, found the perfect partner, or had a more active social life, shame would magically disappear. Unfortunately, that's not how it works. You can dress it in the finest clothes, live in the nicest gated community, and drive the fanciest cars, but none of these material possessions will make shame go away. Overcoming shame is not about the accrual of achievements or relationships or even checking off the boxes on some magical checklist. Defeating shame starts with how you see yourself. It's an in-side job.

Imagine you've just landed your dream job, the one with the corner office, a hefty paycheck, and all the perks you could im-agine. You feel on top of the world—for a while. But then, those familiar feelings of inadequacy start creeping back in. The job didn't magically erase your shame. Think about that perfect relationship you've al-ways wanted. The one who completes you and makes you feel whole. It's a beautiful fantasy, but no person can make you whole or fill the void created by shame. Here's the thing: shame has a way of seep-ing through even the most fortified walls of external success.

When I was a kid, I always wanted a strong bond with my dad. I'd see other boys hanging out with their dads and wished that could be us. However, it wasn't that simple. See, my dad had a wife and two daughters. My mom was always upfront with me about it. For a long time, his wife and my sisters didn't even know I existed. It was a confusing and painful situation.

It was a strange dynamic, because dad would only visit me alone, and those visits were always short. I often wondered why I couldn't spend time with my sisters or why I wasn't invited to holidays. While my dad's wife and daughters had no clue I existed, his mother and siblings knew. Sometimes, dad would take me to visit his mother, and over the years, I managed to build a relationship with my paternal grandmother, even if our visits were few and far between.

Fast forward to when my grandmother passed away. My mom took me to the funeral, and I remember sitting in the back of the funeral home while my dad sat at the front with his family. It was one of the most awkward and painful moments of my life. I was in the same room as my sisters, but I couldn't say a word to them because, well, I was a secret—I didn't exist.

Years after my grandmother's funeral, my mom told me I'd be spending Thanksgiving with my dad and his family. Whoa! This was huge! I was finally going to meet my dad's wife and my sisters. By then, I was in high school at Duke Ellington School of the Performing Arts. I was a straight-A student, an accomplished pianist and vocalist, singing background vocals with the High School Showcase Choir for top R&B and Gospel artists. Not to mention, I was also directing church choirs and playing the organ. You could say I was doing big things. I was grateful for the many opportunities afforded to me.

Thanksgiving Day rolled around, and even though I was a bundle of nerves and had no idea what to expect, I was pumped to meet my new family. The day turned out better than I could have imagined. My sisters and I spent time getting to know each other, and it was the beginning of a very special bond. Here's the thing, despite all my accomplishments and this new family dynamic, those feelings of shame didn't just disappear. I kept wondering if I could meet their expectations, assuming they had any at all. Would they accept me? Maybe they just wanted to get to know their brother, nothing more, nothing less. My mind was flooded with questions.

Shame isn't something you can outrun or out-achieve. It's rooted deeply in fear based on our past experiences and societal expectations. While it's tempting to believe external validation will heal these wounds, the truth is, it won't.

Even though my dad apologized for keeping me a secret from his family for so long, I couldn't shake my feelings about the whole situation. Like I said before, getting over shame isn't about achievements or relationships. It starts with how you see yourself. Understand that you are enough, just as you are. Your worth doesn't come from outside achievements or relationships. It comes from within.

Over time, my relationship with my dad transformed into something I never imagined we could achieve. The same goes for my connection with my sisters and bonus mom. I deeply love my dad and cherish the connection we now have. If you feel like your relationship with your loved one is beyond repair, remember that God can breathe new life into it. God can help you reclaim, restore, and make up for lost time and missed opportunities.

When we abide in Christ, we're wrapped in His righteousness. Think of it like a quick spiritual wardrobe change. This new outfit is designed to kick shame out of your life. You're now wearing what Christ says about you. His words are powerful, and they'll redefine your self-worth. What happens if we flipped the script? Instead of focusing on our perceived flaws and failures, we choose to see the positive qualities within us. It's like looking in a mirror, but instead of pointing out that pimple on your forehead, you start noticing how awesome your smile is.

You Are More Than Your Mistakes

Hey, we all mess up. It's part of being human. But guess what? Those slipups don't define who you are. Jesus knew about your past, future and every little trip-up you'd have even before you turned to Him. What's important to remember is that your identity in Christ is rock solid, despite your flaws. Some folks might say, "I'm a sinner saved by grace," but you can't be both a sinner and saved at the same time. If you call yourself a "sinner," you continue to identify with sin as your way of life. However, being saved means you might mess up sometimes, but sin isn't your go-to anymore. Now, your new life is rooted in God's Word, transforming you into God's righteousness through your faith in Jesus. Remember, "If any man be in Christ, he is a new person, the old has passed and everything is new."[17]

We often accept sayings passed down to us without a second thought, which often fuel our feelings of guilt and shame. However, the good news is that God's Word promises us His redemption and forgiveness. When we stumble, we have a High Priest who's always ready to listen, forgive and clean up our messes.

Your true identity is found in Christ, not in your mistakes or what others think about you. This truth is grounded in the fact that our lives are hidden with Christ in God. Being in God means He's the one who defines who we are. [18] We don't need to hustle for our identity in Christ. All we have to do is embrace what God has already made us. There's no better place to be than resting in this truth.

Getting a new identity in Christ is an incredible gift we shouldn't take for granted.

Sin is sin, no doubt about it. However, our sins don't disqualify us from receiving this new identity, and nor can we try to earn it through good works or actions. In reality, because of God's grace, all we need is faith in His unwavering faithfulness. Our main job is to build our faith and trust in His promises, knowing His faithfulness surpasses our failures. Our efforts will never match the amazing sacrifice God has made for us.

Don't Let Shame Dictate How You Treat Others

Without knowing it, we can come across people who carry a lot of shame from the tough times they've experienced. Unfortunately, our reactions can sometimes add to their shame instead of helping them heal. The Bible encourages us to confess our wrongdoings to one another,[19] and then remind each other of God's endless grace.

A true messenger of God's grace shouldn't zero in on someone's specific mistakes. Instead, they should always emphasize the unconditional love and forgiveness God offers, regardless of past actions. The grace we extend to others is the same grace we rely on ourselves. God's grace in full operation like this would foster a church community flowing in His love, compassion, understanding, and support.

Take the story of the Prodigal Son in Luke 15. Consumed by shame, he decided to go back home after squandering his inheritance. He believed that he no longer deserved to be called a son. So he had already made up his mind to beg for forgiveness and settle for being a servant.

When he returned home and started confessing his sins, his father didn't shame him or even bring up his wrongs. Instead, the father celebrated his son's return by dressing him in fine clothes and throwing a feast, restoring him to his rightful place as a son. This parable reminds us that our heavenly Father isn't concerned with how far we've strayed. We just need to show we want to come back. It's amazing to know we have a Father who will never turn us away.

What if the father in the story had been so bogged down by his own shame because of his son's actions or for any other reason. He wouldn't have been able to reconcile with his son. People who can't confront their own shame often struggle to restore others. They miss the chance to heal themselves and help others because they can't get past their own issues. In short, address your own shame, and don't let it hold you back from offering grace and restoration to others

Freedom from Shame Comes through Christ, Not People

I'm here to tell you that true freedom comes through Jesus, not through anyone else. Listen to these words: "As it is written, Behold, I lay in Sion a stumbling stone and rock of offense: and whosoever believeth on him shall not be ashamed."[20] This means if you believe in Jesus, you won't have to carry any shame. His redemptive power shields us from the shame the enemy throws your way. The enemy often targets our faith because without believing in Jesus as our Savior, shame sticks around like an unwelcome guest.

Understand your true worth. Your value isn't dictated by your social, economic, marital, or financial status. I don't care if you're single, married, rich, or struggling to make ends meet—you are enough! Freedom from shame comes through what Christ says about you, not what people say.

Here's how things began to change in my life. I started seeing myself in a new light, appreciating my worth beyond what I've achieved, what I own, or who I know. It's not about being cocky. It's about knowing you have value just as you are. I decided not to live by others' labels or opinions. I view my life as God does. He planned it out, and I'm following His plan for me with no apologies about it. My birth circumstances, childhood embarrassments, and mistakes don't define me. I know who I am. I'm a man, made in God's image, loaded with purpose and destiny, unapologetically me with no fear of my past. I'm not fazed by what people think of me. I am free from societal or religious constraints.

I am KENNETH WESLEY CHISM. I live without shame and reject any negative thoughts that would try to disturb my peace.

Defeating shame is a journey, but it's one worth taking. By recognizing that your worth comes from Christ and not from external accomplishments or validations, you can break free from the chains of shame. Remember, you are enough. Now go out there and live like it!

7

BEATING SHAME AT ITS GAME

Growing up, I was obsessed with Superman. Watching Clark Kent transform from an everyday reporter into a superhero was magical to me. However, even Superman had his Achilles' heel—kryptonite. That green, glowing rock could bring him to his knees in seconds. Fortunately, he had a secret weapon, his K-Suit, which was made of lead-lined titanium. It protected him from the devastating effects of kryptonite.

Now, let's switch gears a bit. We've been talking throughout this book about how shame shows up uninvited, invades our lives, and refuses to leave. It's like an annoying houseguest who just won't take the hint. Well, here's a little secret. There is a way to defeat shame. That's right, just like Superman, we aren't left defenseless. We have our own kind of lead suit—the Word of God.

Let's get real for a moment. Life isn't a comic book. Sometimes it feels like shame is winning. However, every time you read, memorize, and speak God's Word, you're putting on your lead suit in order to stand strong against the kryptonite of shame.

Suiting Up with the Word of God

Picture this. You're Clark Kent, living your everyday life. Challenges pop up—work

stress, personal doubts, past mistakes—
you name it. Then you remember your secret weapon. You suit up in the armor of
God and swing His Word like a sword.
Suddenly, shame doesn't stand a chance.
Its power fades away, leaving you
stronger and more confident. Think about
it. Ephesians 6:11 says, "Put on the full armor of God, so that you can take your
stand against the devil's schemes." These
aren't just fancy words. They are your spiritual defense mechanism, your K-Suit
against shame. Every time shame tries to
invade your thoughts, remind yourself of
God's promises. Speak them out loud if
you have to. Declare that you are fearfully
and wonderfully made, that there is no
condemnation for those who are in Christ
Jesus, [21] and you are more than a con-
queror. [22] I hope you really believe this!

Shame doesn't stand a chance when we use the Word of God. Yep, you read that right. The Word of God will counteract every lie. It's our spiritual armor, our divine lead suit shields us from the debilitating power of shame. This isn't just some feel-good advice. The Word of God is practical and powerful. You're not just reading some book. You're gearing up for the battle of your life. And guess what? With God's Word as your shield and sword, you've already won.

Superman might be fictional, but the battle against shame is all too real. Thankfully, we don't have to face it unarmed. The Word of God equips us with everything we need to stand firm. It's our lead suit, our protection, and our power.

Using the Word of God to Deal with Shame

Dealing with shame is no walk in the park, but one guaranteed way to win the fight against shame is by trusting in the Word of God. It is a powerful antidote to shame. While shame makes you feel like you're not good enough, God's Word says the exact opposite. Remember, "If we confess our sins, He is faithful and just to forgive us and cleanse us from all unrighteousness."[23] And yes, all means all!

God's Word reminds us that He is gracious, compassionate, slow to anger, and overflowing with mercy. This should motivate us to draw closer to Him, especially when we slip up. There's no need to hide in shame when we can approach our loving Father and seek His forgiveness and guidance. Let's not get it twisted. Our best

defense against shame is God's Word, period. While attending church and listening
to sermons is beneficial, we must actively
declare and proclaim God's promises in
our lives. By affirming our identity in
Christ with statements like, "I am the righteousness of Christ Jesus," we align
ourselves with God's Word and unlock its
transformative power. Knowing God's
Word deeply empowers us to confidently
speak His promises into our lives.

Choose to Believe the Word of God

In a world where self-doubt, past mistakes, and shame can feel like a constant
battle, choosing to believe in the Word of
God is a powerful act of faith and defense.
It's not just about hearing the words. It's
about believing them and letting them
transform the way we live. The Word of

God can be an unshakeable defense—if we genuinely believe it.

One of Satan's favorite tactics is attacking our belief in God's Word. Ever had a nagging thought that your mistakes were too big for God to handle? Yep, that's a classic move from the enemy's playbook. He wants to keep you feeling isolated in your shame and thinking there's no way out. Or maybe you believe in God's Word, but a part of you doubts if He will do it for you because of your past mistakes. It's self-doubt whispering, "Sure, God can do miracles, but not for someone like me." It's like saying, "I believe, but help my unbelief."[24] This is a struggle many of us face, believing in general, but needing help in the area where we specifically struggle to believe.

It's incredibly easy to hear the Word of God and get all pumped up. You walk out of church or close your Bible app feeling like you can conquer the world. Here's real truth. Hearing alone isn't even enough. We are encouraged to take it further: "But be doers of the word, and not hearers only."[25] If we think simply hearing the Word is all we need to do, we're fooling ourselves. It's like signing up for a gym membership and expecting to get fit without actually working out. You've got to put action behind what you've heard. You've got to be willing to work the Word to see real change in your life.

The enemy knows God's Word is your most potent defense. He'll do anything to make you doubt everything God has said about you. Worse yet, he wants you to be clueless about your identity in Christ. Satan knows that if you don't know who you are in Christ, you won't realize the power and authority you have.

Satan thrives on our ignorance and self-doubt. But when we choose to believe the Word of God, we strip him of his power. We start to see ourselves as God sees us—redeemed, loved, and capable of overcoming shame or any past mistake. Believing in the Word of God isn't passive. It's active, dynamic, and sometimes downright challenging, but the rewards are worth it. When you choose to believe, you're not just accepting God's promises, you're also stepping into them. You're allowing His Word to reshape your identity and your reality.

You've got to have a plan to win! Every morning when you wake up, start your day by speaking God's promises over your life. Say them out loud so you can hear them—and the devil too! Memorizing Scripture is also important. Make flash cards with scriptures that speak directly to your struggles and doubts. So, when the enemy attacks, you'll already have a ready defense. Spending time in prayer, asking God to strengthen your belief in His Word, and staying focused on Him are also sure weapons of defense. Choosing to believe the Word of God is a daily decision, especially for those battling shame and self-doubt. It's not always easy, but it's undoubtedly powerful. Remember, God's Word is not only your defense but also your declaration of who you are in Him.

The Power of Prayer

While God's Word is your go-to defense, prayer is your secret weapon. If you're thinking, "But I don't really know how to pray," don't sweat it. Think of prayer as your direct line to the Almighty. It's not just a monologue. It's a two-way conversation with God. And trust me, God wants to hear from you because He has some pretty awesome things to say about you. Through prayer, you allow His voice to become louder and drown out any negative thought or feeling.

Negative thoughts are like those annoying pop-up ads that always interrupt your browsing experience. Your prayers are the ad-blockers you need to shut those negative thoughts down. When shame starts whispering lies, counteract it by praying the truth of God's Word. For example, if you feel unworthy, pray something like, "God, thank You for Your love and acceptance. Help me to see myself through Your eyes."

One of the most effective ways to pray is by using Scripture. It's like having a cheat sheet for life. When you pray God's Word, you're aligning your thoughts with His truths, and it leaves no room for shame. If you're dealing with feelings of inadequacy, pray verses like Philippians 4:13— "I can do all things through Christ who strengthens me."

We've all had moments when we've felt overwhelmed by shame. Personally, I've found combining God's Word with prayer is a game-changer. It's not about having the perfect words or spending hours in solitude. It's about being honest with God and letting His truths reshape your perspective.

Ready to tag-team shame with God's Word and prayer? Start by putting your faith into action today. Speak the Word, believe it, and engage in heartfelt conversations with God. You're not just beating shame. You're transforming your life.

8

SHAME: DEAL OR NO DEAL?

Shame is a tricky emotion which can profoundly impact our lives. When shame creeps in, it's important to deal with it right away. Yet, many of us choose to sweep it under the rug, allowing it to take up even more emotional space. But why do we avoid dealing with it? Perhaps it's because we don't fully understand its source. If we could pinpoint its origin, we would likely feel more empowered to confront it and kick it out of our lives for good.

THE UNINVITED GUEST

To really get to the bottom of it, know that shame can come from all sorts of places. There are four main sources of shame: making honest mistakes, being a victim, inherited shame, and sin. By understanding the sources of our shame, we can learn to identify them and start overcoming shame.

Four Origins of Shame

1. Making Honest Mistakes

We all make mistakes. It's just part of being human. But sometimes these mistakes become a source of shame when we internalize them and believe they define us. Shame isn't always about doing something wrong on purpose or making a huge blunder. It can also come from innocent, accidental slipups. Maybe you sent an email to the wrong person, tripped in front of a crowd, or showed up at a formal event

— 110 —

dressed in casual clothes. At first, you might feel embarrassed, but the more you dwell on that cringe-worthy moment, the more it can turn into a deeper feeling of shame.

This kind of shame usually comes from within us rather than from others. It's closely tied to your self-image. When you mess up unintentionally, those feelings of shame are often driven by your inner thoughts and how you interpret the situation. It's about how you see yourself after the incident and how you think others see you.

Your self-esteem plays a big role in whether embarrassment turns into shame. People with lower self-esteem are more likely to feel shame from these unintentional actions because they are more sensitive to self-criticism and negative self-talk. If you have low self-esteem, you may think the accidental action confirms your negative beliefs about yourself, making the shame feel even worse.

Also, the shift from embarrassment to shame is often fueled by internalized societal standards and expectations. We often judge ourselves harshly based on these norms, even if the slipup was accidental. This internal judgment makes the action seem more significant and it only magnifies the shame.

In short, moving from embarrassment to shame after an unintentional goof-up is related to how you see yourself and the standards you've absorbed. Understanding this can help us better manage those feelings.

Here's how you manage it. First, own it! Acknowledge your mistake instead of hiding it. It takes the power away from shame. Then, use it as a learning experience to determine what you can do differently next time. When all else fails, laugh it off. Sometimes, a little humor goes a long way. Laughing at yourself can lighten the mood and ease the shame.

2. Victimization

This one's tough. When we've been hurt or wronged by others, it can lead to feelings of shame. It's unfair and can create a vicious cycle of self-blame. When people face abuse, rape, or discrimination, it really messes with their self-esteem and brings up a ton of shame.

Victims often start blaming themselves and start believing the negative voices in their heads. They might even start believing the awful things their abusers or society say about them. This can make them think they deserved the mistreatment, which just makes the shame deeper. This kind of internal shame is very harmful because it eats away at their self-worth and keeps them feeling powerless. In some instances, victims are blamed or shunned, making them feel even worse. The fear of judgment or disbelief can make them hide their experiences, which means more isolation and shame.

When I was a little boy, my mom would take me to a local establishment owned by a highly respected man in our community. He had this massive jar of candy on his desk. Seriously, who can say no to candy? He'd pick me up, sit me on his lap, and hand over the candy jar. Sounds innocent enough, right?

When I was about 12, I got a part-time summer job working for him. My tasks were pretty simple—opening boxes, stocking shelves. Nothing too heavy. That same candy jar was still on his office desk, and he'd offer me candy every now and then. To be clear, I wasn't a little kid anymore. No need to sit on your lap, sir, thank you very much.

One day, as I reached for some candy, he touched me in a way that was unfamiliar to me. It was inappropriate, and I didn't know how to respond. I didn't know whether to scream, yell, or cry. I left his office and tried to go on with my work, but I couldn't shake off what had just happened. By the end of the day, I knew I wasn't coming back to work for him.

When I got home, my mom noticed something was wrong and asked about my day.

I just told her I didn't like the job and didn't want to return. How could I explain to her what had happened? I didn't even know how to make sense of it for myself. I knew it felt wrong, but I kept wondering what did I do to deserve this. It made me start questioning the intentions of other men in my life and even myself.

Little did I know, this experience planted a seed of doubt about my sexuality. Was there something wrong with me? And just like that, the fear of being judged or doubted silenced me, leaving me to deal with the hurt all by myself.

Dealing with the aftermath of victimization is incredibly tough. You often wrestle with feelings of guilt, fear, and anger, which only add to the shame. You might feel guilty for not stopping the abuse or think you somehow played a part in it.

Fear of more harm can make you too ashamed or scared to seek help or talk about what happened.

Don't suffer in silence. Find support by talking to someone you trust about your experiences. Sometimes, just being heard can be incredibly helpful and kickstart the healing process. Remind yourself that what happened is not your fault. Be kind to yourself and practice self-compassion. Focus on regaining control of your life, and make choices that support your well-being.

3. Inherited Shame

Ever felt ashamed for something that's not even your fault? Welcome to inherited shame. This can come from family expectations, cultural norms, or societal pressures. Inherited shame often stems from the actions or beliefs of others and can be deeply ingrained. Everyone is unique in their own way, with characteristics that make them special. Sadly, many people struggle to embrace their uniqueness and instead feel ashamed of some of their innate traits. It could be a birthmark, a funny-sounding voice, or maybe they think they're not the right height, weight, or size. Some might feel uncomfortable about their skin tone, whether it's too dark or too light. Others might carry the weight of their family's reputation, like a relative who is a criminal. This could trigger feelings of shame even though it's beyond their control.

This kind of internal shame can seriously damage self-esteem and overall well-being. It can make you feel like you're never good enough. It's important to remember that everyone has their own special qualities and imperfections. By letting go of the shame tied to inherited traits or circumstances, it becomes easier to begin appreciating and celebrating your own uniqueness without being held back by other's opinions.

Here's how to tackle inherited shame. First, identity the source of this same. Is it really yours, or has it been imposed on you? Challenge it and question these inherited beliefs. Does this truly align with your values? Finally, create your own path. Define your own standards by God's Word and live according to them, not someone else's expectations.

4. Our Sins

Finally, for many Christians, sin can be a big source of shame. The feeling of having fallen short and disappointing God can be overwhelming. One of the biggest tricks

the enemy uses is making us feel too unworthy to approach God when we mess
up. The enemy whispers lies, telling us we
are too far gone to be accepted by Him.
He'll even taunt us, saying, if we truly
loved God, we wouldn't keep struggling
with the same sins every week. This kind
of torment often leaves us to feeling that in
order to get back in God's good graces, we
must work tirelessly, with no guarantee
He'll welcome us. These are exactly the
feelings I experienced.

At age 19, I attended a revival service led
by a well-known evangelist. Near the end,
the preacher invited those struggling with
sin to come to the altar—so I went. Deep
down, I've always wanted to please God
and live a holy life. The preacher told us to
think about our sins. He asked us to turn
around three times, saying we will never
face those struggles again. I followed his

instructions to a tee and left the altar feeling like, "Yes! This is behind me now." Before the week ended, I found myself repenting again for the very thing I thought I had conquered. Wait, that prayer didn't work. Did I do something wrong? It became hard for me to pray. Is the Lord mad at me? Is He even listening to me? My doubt and disbelief made it extremely difficult to receive God's forgiveness.

Listen, my friend, this is how the enemy wants you to think. This lie of thinking God has abandoned you because of your sins creates a nasty cycle to trap us deeper in them. We sin, feel ashamed, and distance ourselves from God, thinking we're too bad to be loved or forgiven. If you're not careful, your sin will consume you and cause you to give up on yourself, life, or even God. Satan is a liar! Where do we turn when stuck in this cycle? The answer is in the very place we think we're unwelcomed—in God's arms. He's not a distant judge waiting for us to earn His favor. He's a loving Father who wants us to come to Him, no matter how dirty or broken we feel. His grace isn't limited by our shortcomings. It's boundless and unconditional. We can find the forgiveness, healing, and restoration we need in His presence. Through His love, we can break free from the chains of sin and shame and find the strength to start fresh. Don't believe the enemy's lies anymore. Sin can be a source of shame, but don't let that shame drive you from God. Run to Him. He's waiting with open arms to receive you, just as you are.

Shame is a tricky beast and sneaks up in all sorts of ways. These four main sources of shame are just some examples, but there's always a new tactic to be wary of. Satan's goal is to hold you prisoner to cycles of despair and guilt. He wants to steal your joy and gratitude towards God. However, pinpointing the origins of your shame makes it easier to overcome that shame.

9

SHAME-FREE ZONE

Welcome to the pivotal moment of our journey together. This is where all the insights, reflections, and strategies I have shared with you thus far come together. Now it's time for you to reclaim your life. Close your eyes. Imagine living a life where shame no longer holds you hostage—a reality where you live freely, unburdened by its weight. Sounds like a dream, right? Well, it's time to roll up your sleeves, make this dream a reality, confront shame head-on, and evict it from your life for good. Sure, it may be hard to believe now, but trust me—it's possible. Think of this as your personal shame-free zone.

First off, let's get one thing straight. God cares deeply about your challenges, and so do I. We've talked about everything from unexpected humiliations to feeling like a failure. I mean for real…the tea has been spilled. Guess who's unbothered? Me! While I wrote this book to liberate you and provide you with an action plan, writing has provided another layer of healing to my life. Revelation 12:11 nails it: "And they overcame him by the blood of the Lamb, and by the word of their testimony." So, look out for the next book by this bestselling author.

Take a moment to acknowledge your survival. It's a testament of your strength and resilience. If there's one takeaway from this book, it's that your worth is not defined by the situations you've faced.

Your true identity is anchored in a relationship with Jesus Christ. He offers love, acceptance, and a fresh start. Living in your shame-free zone requires you to make a conscious effort to shame-proof your life.

The Mysterious Intruder

I've mentioned a lot about the uninvited guest, right? However, I never imagined I'd have an uninvited visitor making itself at home in my attic. It all started with strange noises in the night, footsteps scurrying across the ceiling that disrupted my sleep. This mysterious presence was unsettling, and I knew I had to take action.

After hearing these noises over and over, I called wildlife control for an inspection.

What they found was both surprising and slightly amusing. A squirrel had somehow entered my home and had set up camp in the attic. The experts suggested a few immediate steps to fix the situation. First, seal up the foundation by closing any gaps and cracks to stop rodents from entering. Next, set up rodent traps in the attic to catch our furry intruder. Finally, install dryer wall vents to pest-proof the dryer, bathroom, and kitchen vents. These actions were essential to make sure no more unwanted guests would disturb my peace.

Stay with me, I'm going somewhere. Reflecting on this experience, I realized it was more than just dealing with getting rid of a squirrel. It became a metaphor for life. Sometimes, we allow unwanted thoughts and lies to invade our minds, disrupting our peace and holding us captive. It's essential to identify these intrusions and take deliberate actions to seal them out. Just as I took steps to prevent the squirrel from reentering, it is important for us to seal up the cracks in our lives that invite shame and lies. This means installing mental and emotional safeguards by sealing up the foundation, strengthening our sense of identity and self-worth to keep negative thoughts at bay. Set traps for lies by spotting and challenging the false stories that hold you back. And finally, build a protective barrier by setting boundaries to guard your peace and maintain your integrity.

This isn't just about wishing shame away. It's about being kinder to yourself. Cut yourself some slack. We all make mistakes, and that's okay. Show yourself the same understanding and forgiveness you would show a loved one. Allow yourself to feel your emotions, process them, and then let them go. This may involve seeking support from trusted individuals or professionals.

Creating a Shame-Free Zone Starts with Openness

Being open and honest with yourself is so important. You can't just sweep your past under the rug. Acknowledging it is the first step to healing. Get real and face the facts. Trust is another biggie when it comes to squashing shame. Shame's whole game is to make you mistrust others. Ever heard someone say, "I don't trust anyone"? Well, that's unfortunate because without trust, you're unable to get the help you need from others whom God may have assigned to your life. Take that first step and talk to someone, whether it's a trusted spiritual advisor or a therapist.

As I mentioned earlier, my pastor, Apostle Nelson, guided me through the process of recognizing and overcoming shame. It's true. You can't pour your heart out to just anyone. However, there's someone out there meant to support you. Be open to God leading you to the right person who can be helpful.

Trust the Process of Therapy

A great place to start is therapy, especially if you don't have a trusted confidant. Therapy provides you with an opportunity to talk with an unbiased professional. I get it. Bringing up therapy can be tricky, especially in church circles, but hear me out. Therapy and faith are like peanut butter and jelly. They just go together. Therapy was invaluable for me in working through my feelings and experiences. Seeking out a therapist doesn't show a lack of faith.

Quite the contrary. It actually shows you have faith. God gave us these tools for a reason, right? Think of it this way: therapy can help you better communicate your needs to God in prayer. It can provide clearer direction on what to pray for. Remember, being vulnerable isn't a sign of weakness. It's a strength. By opening up, we find the support we need and the courage to move forward.

Living with Purpose

You have a divine purpose and destiny to fulfill. Your presence in this world is not a mere coincidence. God included you deliberately in His blueprint. We are His masterpiece, crafted with a specific purpose in mind, even before we entered our mother's womb.

This understanding should empower us to serve others by using our gifts and talents to help and uplift those around us. We are called to advance the greater good by contributing to the betterment of society and the realization of a higher plan. It's time to break the shackles of shame and live a life that matters.

When we acknowledge we are part of something greater, we can release the hold that shame has over us. The other side of shame is liberation, empowerment, and a life filled with meaning. Living in purpose makes us agents of change, transforming not only our lives but also the world around us. This enables us to step boldly into our purpose and become the masterpiece we were always meant to be. That's what a shame-free zone is all about. It's like getting divine permission to be your real, unapologetic self—minus the judgment and fear.

When God restores, He does it fully and completely. Restoration goes beyond just fixing what's broken. It's about living out God's true intentions for your life with clarity. God never intended for us to carry things He didn't give us. Shame isn't from Him. It's from the enemy. This is where we draw the line. It's time to kick shame and its nasty friends—guilt, condemnation, defeat—right out the door, in Jesus' name.

Get Your Life Back

God delights in and excels at repairing what's been broken, destroyed, or stolen. He loves us deeply and eagerly wants to put the pieces back together, making us whole again. Sure, shame might have stolen some of your precious time, leaving you to hide in its shadows. However, take comfort in this promise from God: "I'll give back the years you lost to hardships and setbacks, whether they came as relentless challenges or overwhelming burdens." He doubles down on this by saying, "You'll have plenty and live a life of abundance, and you'll never feel ashamed again." By holding onto the powerful promise in Joel 2, you can reclaim your life. These words from your loving Father assure you that He'll not only restore you but also lift the heavy weight of shame from your life for good.

Forget the Past and Reach Forward

Paul, who once had a reputation for persecuting Christians, experienced a life-changing transformation after his encounter with Christ. Despite his troubled history, he became a leading figure in the early Christian church. In his letters, he underscores the importance of letting go of the past and fully stepping into the new life offered by Christ.

This shift is evident in 2 Corinthians 7:2 where Paul declares that he has harmed no one and done nothing wrong, showcasing his renewed identity in Christ. In Philippians 3, Paul digs even deeper into this theme. He stresses the need to forget what is behind and focuses on what's ahead.

Paul's message is a powerful reminder for us to release our past mistakes, regrets, and failures to fully engage with the new life and purpose God has in store. By following Paul's example of moving past the old and reaching forward, we too can experience the freedom and grace that comes from living in Christ.

Can you imagine if I had allowed the pain of my past to hinder the possibilities of my future? You wouldn't be reading this book and so many people would have missed out on the impact of my story. My story is a testament to overcoming shame and finding purpose beyond pain. Had I believed the lies of the enemy, I would never have been obedient to God's calling to start one of the greatest reflections of heaven on earth: Restoration House International. Today, I am honored to serve as the founder and servant leader of an amazing church where people are loved, embraced for who they are, and restored to God's true intentions for their lives.

Whoever said you can't pastor effectively and be single obviously hasn't met me! Look at this guy, knocking it out of the park and setting new standards. Yes, it comes with its challenges, but being single hasn't stopped me from making a real impact; in fact, it's been a blessing in disguise, giving me the focus and drive to lead with passion and authenticity.

So, take a cue from Apostle Paul and leave shame behind. Always remember, you're enough just the way you are, and your worth comes solely from Christ. Don't fall for the enemy's lies. Your experiences have shaped you, but they don't define your destiny. Move forward with unwavering confidence, knowing God has amazing plans for you! Your adventure is right in front of you. Let's seize it and make a real impact.

FINAL WORDS

Initially, I decided to write about overcoming shame because, when I was struggling, I couldn't find a book that speaks to my experiences. I wanted to create a guide for others who were hurting, leading them toward a life free from shame.

Before writing this book, I had to come to terms with my own experiences. Whether I shared my story or not, I realized it was okay. Every experience from my past has brought me to where I am now. Nothing is wasted, and I have gained more than I have lost.

Along my journey to living a shame-free life, I discovered my true self. Today, there are no more questions over my head about who I am. No more voices yelling from the past. I am a man created in the image of God, and yes, I am enough…confident and unbothered by the opinions of people.

By the time I sat down to write this book, I had one clear goal: to help people identify and evict shame. Even in the process of writing, shame had the nerve to sneak in with doubts like, "Am I oversharing? What will people think?" Ha! Nice try, shame, but I wasn't having any of it. I smacked shame in the face, shut those thoughts down, and kept on writing. Shame will never silence me or make me hide. Each time I tell my story, I feel even more empowered to live my purpose without worrying about others' opinions.

Robert Frost once said, "I am not a teacher, but an awakener." I hope this book has awakened you to the idea that you have the power to evict shame from your life. Go ahead, kick shame out and start living a life free of shame today.

As we conclude, remember, this isn't the end of your story—it's merely the beginning of a new chapter. Keep your heart open to God's guidance and continue to walk in the freedom He provides. There are many more stories to be told, lessons to be learned, and victories to be won. Thank you for walking this path with me. Stay blessed, stay hopeful, and always remember, in Christ, you are free from shame.

A Prayer for Release

Before we end our time together, let's agree in prayer to release the burdens of shame and condemnation:

Father, in Jesus' name, I stand on Your Word in Romans 8:1, which says there is no condemnation for those who are in Christ Jesus. I'm so grateful for Your forgiveness, grace, and mercy. Lord, I recognize the burden of shame and condemnation that I've been carrying, and I admit it's too heavy for me. I repent for letting these false feelings overshadow Your redeeming love. I turn away from the enemy's lies and rest in the finished work of Calvary, which has not only redeemed and healed me but also canceled the power of shame in my life. I release the Spirit of truth in my life and reject any lies from the past, present, or future. Thank You for healing every area where shame has wounded me. Thank You for Your promises that bring hope and restoration. I receive this cleansing and forgiveness in Jesus' name. Amen.

About the Author

Kenneth W. Chism is a native of Washington, DC, and the founder and pastor of Restoration House International in the same city. With a strong commitment to global missions, Kenneth dedicates his life to God spreading hope and inspiration across the world.

A multi-talented individual, Kenneth is also a gospel recording artist, singer, and musician. His entrepreneurial spirit drives him to continuously build and uplift the lives of others, reflecting his profound love for God, his family, and community.

Whether through his music, ministry, or missionary work, Kenneth consistently exemplifies a passion for service and a relentless pursuit of making a positive impact on those around him.

END NOTES

[1] Tangney et al., 2007

[2] Tracy & Robins, 2004

[3] Tangney, 1992

[4] Beck, et al., 1985; Gilbert, 1998

[5] Bear, et al., 2009; Bennett, et al., 2005; Harper & Arias, 2004; Paulhus, et al., 2004

[6] Power & Dalgleish, 1997

[7] Sabini & Silver, 1997; Rozin et al., 1999; Miceli & Castelfranchi, 2018

[8] Psalm 139:14

[9] Hebrews 4:15

[10] 2 Corinthians 5:21

[11] Hebrews 12:2

[12] Hebrews 11:6

[13] Numbers 23:19

[14] John 3:16-17

[15] Luke 5:31-32

[16] Galatians 6:1

[17] 2 Corinthians 5:17

[18] Colossians 3:3

[19] James 5:16

[20] Romans 9:33

[21] Romans 8:1

[22] Romans 8:37

[23] 1 John 1:9

[24] Mark 9:24

[25] James 1:22

Made in the USA
Middletown, DE
24 August 2024

59663159R00088